10 Hidden Heroes

by **MARK K. SHRIVER**
New York Times Bestselling Author

Illustrated by
LAURA WATSON

LOYOLAPRESS.

BAKERY

Shoes

GROCERY

PET VET

Bistro

FLOWERS

OPEN

Ten Hidden Heroes
working night and day,
nursing others back to health
until they are okay.

3

9

Nine Hidden Heroes

teaching right and wrong,
making rules to keep us safe
and help us get along.

FIRE DEPARTMENT

TOWN POOL

LIFEGUARD

BEACH

8

Eight Hidden Heroes

find a way to shine,
working hard to save the Earth
one good deed at a time.

7

Seven Hidden Heroes

helping people who are poor,
knowing when you choose to give,
you always get back more.

6

Six Hidden Heroes

teaching others to read.
Getting books in lots of hands,
that is how to lead!

FARM RD.

Save the Children

Save the Children

FREE BOOKS TODAY

11

5

Five Hidden Heroes

guiding us to pray,
giving thanks and praise to God,
helping us find our way.

ice cream

Our
Lady of
Mercy

13

Four Hidden Heroes

inventing with their minds,
rocket ships and medicines,
treasures for humankind!

ice cream

4

Three Hidden Heroes
each with different gifts,
showing us that real success
is when our spirits lift.

ALL WELCOME
WIZARD OF OZ

CENTRAL
middle school
THEATER
SEATING

ICE CREAM HUT

GLASSES

BESTBUDDIES

BESTBUDDIES

2

Two Hidden Heroes
choosing not to fight,
being brave by making peace
and doing what is right.

KiDS for PEACE SUMMIT

1

One Hidden Hero

What is it you will do?

It's your turn to help and heal.

The way? It's up to you!

Special Olympics Israel

Special Olympics United Arab Emirates

Save the Children

Hero Award

Presented To:

For:

Tell how you will be a hero. Draw yourself.

I'm a hero!

1

I'm a hero!

How Many Hidden Heroes Did You See?

10 — Find These Ten Hidden Heroes

1. A girl helping a hurt kitten
2. A boy bringing food to his sick mom
3. A girl putting a cold rag on her sister's forehead
4. A boy putting a bandage on his sister's knee
5. A boy getting a glass of water for his brother
6. A girl taking her little brother's temperature
7. A boy adopting a dog from a shelter
8. A doctor taking a patient's blood pressure
9. A doctor reviewing an X–ray
10. A nurse reviewing a patient's chart

9 — Find These Nine Hidden Heroes

1. A bus driver directing children off the bus
2. A crossing guard helping kids cross the street
3. A police officer giving a child a teddy bear
4. A judge in a courtroom
5. A firefighter installing a child's safety seat
6. An ambulance driver
7. A lifeguard on duty
8. A swim instructor putting floaties on a child
9. A mom applying sunscreen on her daughter

8 — Find These Eight Hidden Heroes

1. A man installing solar panels on a roof
2. Children planting trees
3. A family picking up trash
4. A sanitation worker picking up recycling bins
5. A woman planting a garden
6. A man composting fruits and vegetables
7. A family riding bikes together
8. A boy refilling his reusable water bottle

7 — Find These Seven Hidden Heroes

1. A boy helping stock shelves at a food bank
2. Children collecting clothes for a clothing drive
3. Children collecting books for a book drive
4. A girl helping build a house for those in need
5. Kids running a 5K for the homeless
6. A girl holding the door
7. A boy saving his allowance for others

Find These Six Hidden Heroes

1. A teacher teaching ABCs in front of a class
2. A parent reading to a child
3. A librarian reading to children during outside story time
4. A girl tutoring kids
5. Save The Children staff members distributing free books
6. Volunteers teaching online classes to prison inmates

5

Find These Five Hidden Heroes

1. A religious sister praying for a baby
2. A rabbi helping a boy practice his Torah reading
3. An imam with a Muslim family
4. A choir singing
5. A Buddhist praying with students

4

Find These Four Hidden Heroes

1. A girl setting off a homemade rocket
2. A boy working on a math problem
3. Women writing computer code
4. A scientist working on an experiment

3

Find These Three Hidden Heroes

1. A boy teaching his friend to paint
2. A child helping others read Braille
3. A girl on crutches directing a fellow actor in the school play

Find These Two Hidden Heroes

1. Special Olympics athletes celebrating together
2. Peace Corp volunteer teaching kids about peace

1

Draw yourself and write how you can be a hero!

10 Hidden Heroes

JOIN THE SEARCH!

Heroes are everywhere—in our neighborhoods,
in our schools, and even in our homes. Who are the heroes in your life?
Join the search and share your stories at
www.10hiddenheroes.com.

Find fun activities and simple ways to shine a light
on the people who do good in your world!

Text © 2021 Mark K. Shriver
Illustrations Laura Watson
All rights reserved.
ISBN: 978-0-8294-5269-3

The name and logo of the Peace Corps is reproduced with the kind permission of the Peace Corps.
www.peacecorps.gov. 🌀 Peace Corps

The name and logo of Special Olympics is reproduced with the kind permission of Special Olympics,
Inc., Washington, DC www.specialolympics.org. Special Olympics

The name and mark of Save the Children 🧒 is reproduced with the kind permission of
Save the Children Federation, Inc. www.savethechildren.org.

The name of Best Buddies is reproduced with the kind permission of Best Buddies International, Inc.
www.bestbuddies.org BEST BUDDIES

Library of Congress Control Number: 2020946572

Printed in USA

20 21 22 23 24 25 26 27 28 29 CGC 10 9 8 7 6 5 4 3 2 1

LOYOLAPRESS.
A JESUIT MINISTRY

3441 N. Ashland Avenue
Chicago, Illinois 60657
(800) 621-1008
www.loyolapress.com